Hearts, Cupids, and Red Roses

HEARTS, CUPIDS,
and
RED ROSES

The Story
of the Valentine Symbols

by EDNA BARTH

illustrated by

URSULA ARNDT

A Clarion Book
THE SEABURY PRESS · NEW YORK

LIBRARY OF CONGRESS CATALOGING IN PUBLICATION DATA

Barth, Edna.
    Hearts, cupids, and red roses.

    SUMMARY: The history of Valentine's Day and the
little-known stories behind its symbols.
    Bibliography: p. 63
    1. St. Valentine's Day—Juvenile literature.
[1. St. Valentine's Day]   I. Arndt, Ursula, illus.
II. Title.
GT4925. B32   394.2′683   73-7128
ISBN 0-8164-3111-6

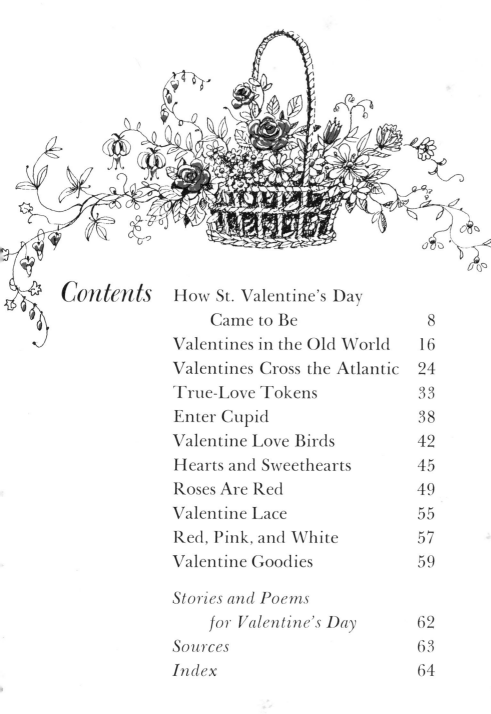

Contents

Cupids with bows and arrows, heart shapes, paper lace, birds, and flowers. All these stand for St. Valentine's Day, just as holly and reindeer stand for Christmas or witches and pumpkins for Halloween.

Some of the Valentine symbols, like a cupid, or a heart pierced with a golden arrow, suggest the holiday all by themselves. Others express it only in combinations. A pair of turtle doves, a cluster of rosebuds, and a heart made of paper lace quickly combine to mean St. Valentine's Day.

Weeks before February 14, the windows of card shops and candy stores display the pretty trimmings and trappings of the coming holiday. Inside are people choosing valentines or buying candy in heart-shaped boxes.

A lighthearted holiday, Valentine's Day is a time when people express feelings of friendship, affection, and love, especially love for someone special.

6

The cupids, the pairs of birds, the flowers
—all the symbols—have to do with love and
courtship. Where each symbol came from and
how it blended with the others forms a fas-
cinating, often lovely story. Some of the stories
have beginnings so ancient they are dim with
time. But each one, like a handmade valentine, can be pieced together.

How St. Valentine's Day Came to Be

Who was St. Valentine, the saint we think of as the patron of lovers? No one seems really sure. Early church records list a number of martyrs by this name. And the feast day of each was February 14.

The St. Valentine of legend is usually described as a priest or bishop who lived in the third century after Christ. According to one legend, he was a Roman priest with a special feeling for young people. When the Roman Empire needed soldiers, Emperor Claudius II decreed that no one could marry or become engaged. Claudius believed that marriage made men want to stay at home instead of fighting wars. The kindly Valentine defied the Emperor's decree and secretly married a number of young couples. He was arrested, imprisoned, and put to death.

Another legend tells of a Valentine who was seized for helping Christians who were being persecuted by Claudius II. During Valentine's time in prison, the jailer and his family were so impressed with his sincerity that they became Christians themselves.

8

This Valentine was especially friendly with the jailer's blind daughter and, by a miracle, restored her sight. The morning of his execution, he is said to have sent her a farewell message signed, "From your Valentine."

Valentine was beheaded on February 14. When he was buried, the story goes on, a pink almond tree near his grave burst into bloom as a symbol of lasting love.

Legends like these are pretty but they fail to explain how the name of a pious churchman became the name for a holiday of love and lovers. This probably came about through twists and turns in the course of history.

February 14, when Valentine is supposed to have died, was the eve of an important Roman festival, the *Lupercalia*. On this evening, Roman youths drew the names of girls who would be their partners during the festival.

Valentine's execution may have formed part of the entertainment during one of these festivals. Roman rulers often made a display of their cruelty toward the Christians who were drawing people away from the older gods.

The Lupercalia festival was an echo of the days when Rome consisted of a group of shepherd folk, living on the hill now known as the Palatine. On the calendar of the time of Valentine, February came later than it does today, so the Lupercalia was a spring festival.

It is thought by some to have once honored *Faunus,* who, like the Greek Pan, was a god of herds and crops. But so ancient is the origin of the festival that even scholars of the last century before Christ were never sure.

About its importance there is no question. Records show, for example, that Mark Antony, an important Roman, was master of the *Luperci* College of Priests. And he chose the Lupercalia festival of the year 44 B.C. as the proper time for offering the crown to Julius Caesar.

Each year, on February 15, the Luperci priests gathered on the Palatine at the cave of *Lupercal.* Here, according to legend, Romulus and Remus, founders of Rome, had been nursed by a mother wolf. In Latin, *lupus* is the word for wolf.

At the door of the cave, several goats and a dog were sacrificed. Then two youths of

noble birth were brought forward. Their foreheads were touched with blood and wiped off with sheepswool dipped in milk.

Now the two youths were supposed to laugh. Then they ran through the Roman streets, lashing about them with goatskin thongs. The streets would be crowded with young women, for a lash of the sacred thongs was believed to make them better able to bear children.

The goatskin thongs were the *februa,* the lashing the *februatio,* both stemming from a Latin word meaning to purify. From it comes our name for February.

The Lupercalia was probably established to ensure good crops, to protect the flocks from wolves, and to keep the animals and their owners healthy and fertile.

Long after Rome had become a walled city and the seat of a powerful empire, the Lupercalia lived on. When Roman armies invaded what are now France and Britain in the first century before Christ, they took the Lupercalia customs there. It is thought that one of these was the drawing of names for partners or sweethearts on February 14.

11

From the teachings of Christ, a new religion was born, and by the fourth century A.D. it was declared lawful. Throughout the Roman Empire the church fathers did their utmost to stamp out everything *pagan,* the name they gave to the older religions. Unable to abolish some of the pagan festivals that people loved, they assigned them Christian names.

So it was with the Lupercalia, which survived late into the 5th century. St. Valentine's name was given to a festival that had celebrated springtime and fertility in human beings and other animals. And, do what the church might, the ancient meaning never quite left it. Memories of the Lupercalia as a celebration of mating were handed down, attaching themselves to the saint's name.

For a time in the Middle Ages, at the Feast of St. Valentine, a spring festival took place in Italy. There, young people gathered in groves and gardens to listen to love poetry and romantic music. Pairing off, they strolled about among the flowers and trees.

The custom died out, however, and there has been no real Valentine's Day celebration in Italy for many years.

In France, too, there were popular forms of pairing off. In one area of the Vosges Mountains, for example, the elders broke up into two groups. One group had a list of young

12

women who wished to marry. The other had a list of young men. From the windows of two houses on opposite sides of a narrow street, they took turns calling out names, in this way forming pairs.

The couples would then meet. If they liked each other, the young woman would prepare a meal, which she and her partner would eat together. Afterward they would go to a Valentine dance.

If a young man disliked his valentine, he would desert her. For eight days she would keep to herself. At the end of that time, the deserter would be burned in effigy at a public bonfire, with the onlookers shouting abuse.

Sometimes a young flirt would be paired with an elderly drunkard—just for "fun."

This sort of celebration left many hard feelings and often led to trouble, and the French government disapproved. In 1776 the pairing customs were finally banned, but here and there they continued into the 1880's. Then, once again, by government order, St. Valentine's Day disappeared in France.

13

Austria, Hungary, and Germany also had St. Valentine's Day courtship customs that have long since vanished. Some of the priests in these countries discouraged them by having the young men draw the names of saints instead of the names of girls. During the year, they were supposed to model themselves after these saints. The custom was not very popular.

In the British Isles it was different. Centuries after the invading Romans left, youths were drawing names for "valentines" or sweethearts on February 14. For a time in the 17th century, while the Puritans were strong in England, St. Valentine's Day was banned. Then, in 1660, with Charles II restored to the throne, the holiday was revived and the drawing of names resumed.

For the well-to-do this became expensive, since the men were expected to give their valentines costly presents. Those lower in the social scale gave simpler gifts. In all classes of English society, there were men who chose St. Valentine's Day to send love tokens, love letters, or proposals to women they truly loved.

By the late 18th century, valentine love letters and handmade love tokens evolved into what we think of as true valentines.

English and German settlers, in the meantime, were bringing memories of Valentine's Day to the New World. There, once the

14

colonies were well-established, handmade love tokens and valentines appeared.

With the 19th century, better printing methods in England and America brought lovely readymade valentines and a growing interest in the holiday. Then, gradually, as machine-made valentines dropped in quality, interest flagged. By the twentieth century it had become mostly a children's holiday, observed in schools.

Not until the 1920's did it revive in England. In the United States, where the printing of cards had suffered from a World War I paper shortage, there was a similar revival.

Since World War II, shops in Germany have stocked valentines for American servicemen stationed there. This, in turn, has renewed German interest in the holiday. In some parts of Germany and in parts of Austria and Spain, it is now observed a little, too, with gifts of candy or flowers.

But it is mainly in the United States and Britain that St. Valentine's Day has been kept alive. In both countries, people of all ages enjoy Valentine parties and the exchange of valentines.

Valentines in the Old World

But for valentine greeting cards, St. Valentine's Day itself might well have vanished. The valentine has kept alive not only the holiday, but most of its symbols.

Valentine was once a word that meant sweetheart. Only gradually did it come to mean a message of love on a piece of paper.

In 15th century England, a French war prisoner, Duke Charles of Orleans, whiled away his time in the Tower of London writing romantic poems. In one of these he spoke of Cupid and St. Valentine.

Another, translated into modern English, begins like this:

> Wilt thou be mine? dear love, reply,
> Sweetly consent, or else deny;
> Whisper softly, none shall know,
> Wilt thou be mine, love? ay or no?

Margery Brews wrote the oldest known valentine in letter form. Dated 1477, it was sent to John Paston, Margery's "Right worshipful and well beloved Valentine."

16

For the next few hundred years, some of England's finest writers wrote valentine poems. In 1648, Robert Herrick addressed his mistress:

Choose me your Valentine,
Next let us marry.

On St. Valentine's Day in 1667, Samuel Pepys described in his famous *Diary* a kind of valentine received by his wife. On a sheet of blue paper her name was written in gold letters by a little boy. This was a forerunner of later valentines.

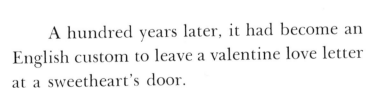

A hundred years later, it had become an English custom to leave a valentine love letter at a sweetheart's door.

Meanwhile, in Catholic countries, religious valentines had begun to appear. Usually made by nuns, they were cut in lacy patterns and decorated with painted flowers. At the center there was often a saint and the sacred heart.

In France and Germany, by the 18th century, friendship or lovers' cards had come into being. They were decorated with borders of flowers, cupids, and birds, and a space was left for a greeting. These were not given on Valentine's Day but at the New Year or on a birthday or anniversary.

The Germans of this time were also making fancy writing paper with similar borders for love letters. Imported into England, it was used for valentine letters.

The German lovers' cards and the fancy writing paper may have helped inspire the valentine that was born in England. The imported paper was expensive, so the British soon began making it themselves. By the late 1700's men in love were sending Valentine love letters or verses on English paper printed with hearts, roses, and cupids.

Before long there were printed folders with space for a message inside. On the front were delicate flowers, leaves, trees, hearts, cupids, love birds, or loving couples. Sometimes in the background, stood a church or a temple of love.

Most of the valentines were sentimental. Others, like those designed by George or Robert Cruikshank, were comic.

The British were proud of their navy, so some of their valentines showed a sailor on board a ship or a sailor enjoying a parting kiss from his sweetheart. Others pictured such events as the appearance of Halley's Comet in 1835.

Those who could wrote their own verses. Others copied verses from booklets called Valentine Writers. In them were special verses for the lovelorn, the lonely, the sick, for the postman, the milkman, the butcher, the baker, or the candlemaker, for people young and old. The verses ranged from the most loving and sincere to "comic" ones that made fun of spinsters or misers.

The verse on one comic valentine meant for a postman went like this:

Haste thee with this Valentine, thou
    silly man of letters,
And try to do the best you can to serve
    and please your betters,
For I'd sooner live an old maid or else
    give up the ghost,
Than wed a grinning postman as
    stupid as a post.

An equally insulting verse intended for a spinster went:

'Tis all in vain your simpering looks,
  You never can incline,
With all your bustles, stays, and curls,
  To find a Valentine.

By 1815 most English towns and cities had a Penny Post. Now, within any one area, mail could be sent cheaply. Soon February 14 became one of the postman's busiest days. The young people of a household waited eagerly for his knock, hoping for at least one valentine. To be passed by was disappointing.

To receive a rude or insulting valentine was still worse. In most places postage was paid by the person receiving the mail. So people who paid the postage on insulting valentines sometimes asked for their money back. A fair-minded postmaster might put on his spectacles and look carefully at such a valentine. If he agreed that it was an insult, he would return the pennies.

PAPER POCKETS
Most valentines were simply folded and sealed with wax. Mail sent in a "paper pocket" or envelope cost twice as much. Sending mail anywhere beyond one's own vicinity cost extra, too.

20

Then, in 1840, a Penny Post was set up for the whole kingdom. With the lower postage, more people used envelopes. Soon, smaller valentine sheets appeared with lovely, decorated envelopes of matching size. Senders folded the envelope flaps themselves, sealing them with wax or with wafers of colored paper, inscribed with mottoes.

THE GOLDEN AGE OF ENGLISH VALENTINES

Anything to do with the time of Queen Victoria, 1837–1901, we call Victorian. Lacy valentines of this era reached their peak in the years 1840–1860. On the delicate paper lace were pasted handpainted motifs—cupids, birds, flowers, hearts, and darts. Some valentines were enhanced with silk, satin, chiffon, net, or real lace.

Novelty valentines might feature a tiny mirror, an envelope, a puzzle purse, or a slot meant to hold a lock of hair. There were valentine checks drawn against the Bank of Love, and valentines printed to look like paper money. One of these looked too much like a real five-pound note and was quickly recalled.

Later on in Victoria's reign, Walter Crane and Kate Greenaway, now famous for their

children's book illustrations, designed valentines.

At twenty-two, Kate Greenaway sold her first design for fifteen dollars. Within a few weeks sales amounted to 25,000 copies. Afterward, for a number of years, she designed others but was never paid a penny more.

Today Kate Greenaway's valentines are collectors' items, as are those designed by Walter Crane. Favorite Greenaway valentines picture charming children dressed in quaint costumes of the previous century.

A FLOOD OF VALENTINES

As the century advanced, more and more valentines came pouring out of workrooms, where young women worked from eight in the morning until seven at night for little pay. *Punch* magazine complained that no sooner had the country recovered from a flood of Christmas cards than it was flooded with "Hearts and Darts and Loves and Doves and Floating Fays [fairies] and Flowers."

It was 1880, and valentines had lost their delicacy. Fringes and tassels replaced the fine lace paper. Many valentines were smothered in feathers, fake flowers, jewels, beads, seeds, and berries.

One English valentine, made to order, consisted of three thousand different pieces. A kind popular with gold miners in Australia was two feet long and came in a box. On it were all sorts of trinkets and gewgaws, including bits of velvet, satin, and swansdown.

There were still lovely English valentines, but many were in such poor taste that people lost interest in them. By the end of World War I, English valentines had become relics of a bygone era.

Then, in 1925, Lady Jeanetta Tuck made a suggestion to her husband, Sir Adolph Tuck, who owned a greeting card business. The firm's Diamond Jubilee was to take place the following year, and Lady Tuck thought it should be celebrated by a revival of the charming old custom of sending valentines.

Her idea was accepted, and the public greeted the new cards with enthusiasm. Other English card makers began producing valentines and have continued to ever since. Today, toward the middle of February, British mails swell as people, young and old, send one another valentine greetings.

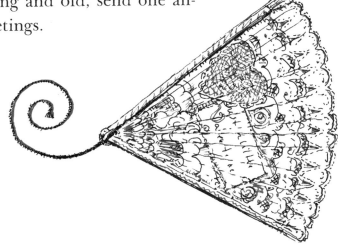

Valentines Cross the Atlantic

On St. Valentine's Day in 1629, John Winthrop wrote a letter to Mrs. Winthrop before leaving England for the New World. It began, "My sweet wife" and ended:

> Thou must be my
> valentine for none
> hath challenged me.

John Winthrop became governor of the Massachusetts Bay Colony. However, there was little room at first in the English colonies for light, flowery occasions like St. Valentine's Day. Ordinary men and women had all they could do to keep themselves and their families alive. Besides, in Puritan strongholds like Plymouth, these things went against the grain.

As far as we know, it was a century or more later that American valentines first appeared. Handmade, with hours of work lavished on them, they were treasured and handed down in families.

Some were made by young suitors, others by skilled artists who traveled about from house to house. Most were sent by men, but now and then a girl sent one, sometimes in reply to one she had received.

The valentines might be decorated in watercolor or in delicate pen and ink. Often the handwriting was a thing of beauty in itself, for fine penmanship was considered a kind of art.

Acrostic valentines had verses in which the first letter of the lines spelled out the loved one's name.

Cutout valentines were made by folding the paper several times and then cutting out a lacelike design with small, sharp, pointed scissors.

Pinprick valentines also had the look of paper lace. These were made by pricking tiny holes in paper with a pin or needle.

Theorem or *Poonah* valentines had designs that were painted through a stencil cut in oil paper, a style that came from the Orient. A coat of gum arabic kept the paint from running.

acrostic

pinprick

Dearest **1**, for you 👁 🌲
Will you 🐝 my Valentine?

Rebus valentines had verses in which tiny pictures took the place of some of the words. An eye might stand for the word I, a heart shape for the word heart.

Puzzle Purse valentines were a puzzle to read and to refold. Scattered among their many folds were verses that had to be read in a certain order.

Fraktur valentines had ornamental lettering in the style of illuminated manuscripts of the Middle Ages.

About three hundred years ago, groups of Germans settled in what is now Pennsylvania. Because the word *Deutsch,* meaning German, sounds something like *Dutch* they have often been called the Pennsylvania Dutch. These German settlers brought the *fraktur* style with them from the Old World.

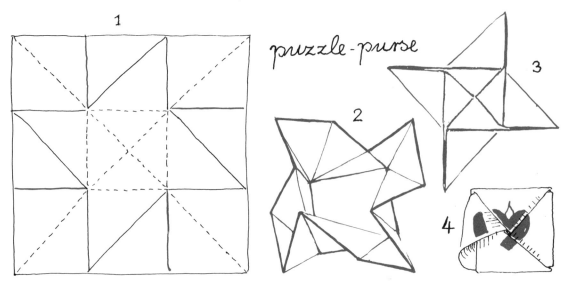

puzzle-purse

1

2

3

4

Today collectors hunt for Pennsylvania German fraktur valentines as well as those done in pen and ink, pinprick, or cutout.

Pennsylvania German valentines are bright and cheerful. On them are birds, hearts, tulips, and angels, painted in fresh reds, blues, greens, and yellows. Usually these valentines were sent as proposals of marriage.

Similar designs decorate the Pennsylvania love tokens, birth or marriage certificates, and other papers. Those unable to read German sometimes mistake them for valentines.

Handmade American valentines continued well into the 1880's, but there were now printed ones as well. These were usually large decorated sheets, with a space for the greeting.

Sailors on voyages sometimes bought their sweethearts a square of silk or other material printed with hearts, cupids, flowers, love knots, and verses. Such a square could be used as a kind of purse or worn as a kerchief, and was known as a bundle valentine.

The sailors themselves carried their belongings in a "bundle" of stronger material. Their sweethearts liked to make them as parting gifts.

By 1840, along with the machine age, came new printing methods and more American valentines. These were engraved, made from woodcuts, or printed, then colored by hand. On them were pictures of lovers, cupids, scrolls, and garlands.

As in England, postage in the United States had been extremely costly. Then, in 1845, one rate was set for the whole country, and the sending of valentines became even more popular.

Many of the new readymade valentines were charming, but expensive. Cheaper ones with crude coloring and cruder verses could also be purchased. The valentine made by hand for a particular person was becoming a thing of the past. The valentine business was booming.

Sentimental valentines might show a couple with a cupid overhead and a coach waiting to take the couple to a church. There were all sorts of novelties, too, including Bank of Love checks. There were also plenty of valentines that ridiculed the old and wrinkled, the drunkard or braggart, or people in various trades. Known as *Vinegar Valentines,* these usually went unsigned. As time went on, these spiteful "comics" made many people lose interest in valentines of any kind.

THOSE FOOLISH NOTES CALLED VALENTINES

In the meantime, Esther Howland, a young woman in Worcester, Massachusetts, started a venture that did a great deal to keep the holiday alive.

It was 1848, and Esther had recently received her diploma from what is now Mount Holyoke College. There the headmistress had warned the students against "those foolish notes called valentines." But Esther, along with many other young people, liked them.

Her father, a stationer, had just imported some lacy English valentines. Struck by their beauty, Esther decided to make some herself. Cutting up some lacy envelopes, she pasted bits of the lace and little colored pictures onto sheets of paper.

The results were so good that her father sent to England for lace paper, colored paper, and paper flowers. Soon Esther had designed a dozen more. Her brother, who was packing his buggy with stationery for a selling trip, took them along as samples.

Dreaming of a few hundred dollars, Esther was stunned when her brother returned with orders worth five thousand dollars! With supplies from England and a group of girls to help her, she set to work in one large room of

her parents' house. Esther designed the cards, and the others copied them. One cut out pictures to be pasted on the valentines. Another made the backgrounds, passing them on to the next person for further decoration. Long before the time of Henry Ford, Esther Howland was using methods of the assembly line.

Orders swiftly mounted and Esther hired more assistants, taking over the entire third floor of her family's house. When this became cramped, she moved her factory to still larger quarters. The young women she hired counted themselves lucky, for it was pleasant work and Esther paid them well.

For several years Esther Howland was the main, if not the only, American maker of lacy valentines. Collectors today sometimes spot Howland valentines by the bright paper disks, known as wafers, that Esther liked to place under the lace. But most collectors look for a small red letter H on the back to identify cards made in her workshops.

Sometime around 1860, Esther Howland went alone to New York City to buy supplies and to see some customers. All over Worcester, tongues began wagging. Women of the time were not expected to take business trips and certainly not alone!

One New York company bought $25,000 worth of Howland valentines every year. And at least one company tried to buy her out. But only many years later, when her aged father needed her, did she sell the business.

VALENTINES AND THE CIVIL WAR

During the war between the North and South there were special valentines for soldiers and their sweethearts. Some showed the lovers' parting. Others had a tent with flaps that opened to reveal a soldier. This was a *window* valentine. In times of peace the "window" was more likely to be a church door, opening on a bride and groom.

Another Civil War novelty was the valentine that included a lock of hair. Still another was the *dressed* or *paper doll* valentine that had a printed face and feet, with the figure dressed in cloth or paper.

After the Civil War, as makers competed for business, American valentines became coarser and gradually more elaborate. Samples from the Gay Nineties have layers of gold, silver, and bronze lace and all sorts of gaudy ornaments.

Novelties of the period included valentines in the form of a fan or a tomato. At that time tomatoes grew only in flower gardens. Considered unfit to eat, they were admired for their beauty and called *love apples*.

31

love apple

By the end of the century the United States was importing goods from countries with cheaper labor. From Germany came brightly colored mechanical valentines. Especially popular were standup automobiles, with pretty girls as passengers and cupids as chauffeurs.

From Germany, too, came valentine postcards. Collecting picture postcards was a popular American hobby and many albums included samples of the valentine postcards.

World War I cut off the supply of German valentines, and a wartime paper shortage reduced the number produced at home.

When the United States entered the war, patriotic valentines appeared. Some of these bore the name of Norcross, a New York greeting card company begun in 1914. Four years earlier, the company now named Hallmark had opened its doors in Kansas City, Missouri. After the war, these and other card companies sold more and more greeting cards, including valentines.

Hallmark and Norcross both have famous collections of antique valentines. Each year, sets of the rare valentines are lent to card shops throughout the country and put on display. Others are in museums and libraries, where they appear in exhibits around St. Valentine's Day.

32

True-Love Tokens

Hearts, cupids, birds, and flowers have
been Valentine symbols for centuries.
Others, just as lovely, have slipped into the
background. Among these is the true-love
knot.

With no beginning and no end, the love
knot consists of graceful loops, sometimes in
the form of hearts. On the loops are endless
love messages that can be read by turning the
knot about.

Love knots were the main design on
many handmade English and American valentines. And, before there were true valentines,
a love knot made of ribbon or drawn on paper
served as a love token. So did paper hearts cut
with pretty designs. A young man would hang
his token on his true love's doorknob, slipping
a love letter under her door.

A popular 19th century love token was a
paper hand. A symbol of courtship, it was

33

probably chosen because a man proposed by asking a lady "for her hand." Like a true-love knot, the lady's hand appeared on handmade valentines and on later printed ones.

Tiny paper gloves were also popular. Real gloves had long been a favorite valentine gift, especially in the British Isles. Among people of fashion, the gloves or other gifts had not always been tokens of real love. They were something a lady expected from a man in her social circle who had drawn her name as his valentine.

Many a wealthy nobleman gave his valentine costly jewels. Others gave what they could. Samuel Pepys, a self-made man, complained bitterly in his famous *Diary* of the high cost of valentine tokens. In addition to gloves, he listed sets of shoestrings, silk stockings, and garters.

For fancy garters were also welcome. One verse sent with a pair of garters begins like this:

Blush not, my fair, at what I send.
'Tis a fond present from a friend.
These garters, made of silken twine,
Were fancied by your Valentine.

Samuel Pepys was not alone in being annoyed by the expense of the gloves, garters, or jewels, and in time valentine gifts became more simple. In some parts of Britain, gloves became true love tokens. Sometimes giving the gloves was a way of proposing. If the girl accepted, she wore them to church the following Easter.

Well into the 1800's, suitors went on giving their sweethearts valentine gloves. With them went verses like this:

> If that from Glove, you take the
>   letter G
> Then Glove is Love and that I send
>   to thee.

In Germany, at this time, Valentine's Day had disappeared as a holiday, but people in love still liked to exchange love tokens. This might be done around Valentine's Day or on a birthday or other occasion.

The Germans who settled in Pennsylvania brought the custom with them. With their flair for design, they created love tokens of lasting beauty. Often a single or double heart, the token might be cut with delicate scissor work or painted with leaves and flowers.

Many girls of the early 19th century gave watchpapers to their sweethearts. Made in the shape of a circle, they replaced the ordinary papers that kept dust out of the cases of pocket watches. Some were made of pretty paper, some of silk or satin. As decoration the girls painted or embroidered designs, perhaps both sweethearts' initials, or a motto. The decorations on some of the papers suggest that they were given at St. Valentine's Day.

VALENTINE'S DAY AT SEA

Many sailors made a hobby of *scrimshaw* —scratching or carving designs on pieces of tusk, bone, or a foreign wood. A scrimshaw piece often became a love token for a wife or sweetheart. Hearts, flowers, leaves, and a pair of doves were all popular as designs. Somewhere on the token was usually a date and the name of a woman.

Long, flat, slender scrimshaw pieces were meant for corset stiffeners. Corsets were known as stays and the stiffeners as busks. One home-

36

sick sailor carved a stay busk with lovely designs and the following message:

> Accept, dear girl, this busk from me
> Carved by my humble hand.
> I took it from a sperm whale's jaw
> One thousand miles from land.
> In many a gale had been the whale
> In which this bone did rest.
> His time is past, his bone at last
> Must now support thy breast.

Handmade love knots; scrimshaw pieces,
lovingly carved and inscribed; gloves, garters,
and other charming Valentine love tokens
have disappeared. One by one, they lost their
meaning or were replaced with articles made
by machines.

Today people are more likely to express
their love with gifts of candy, flowers, jewelry,
or perfume. Usually the gift is given by the
boy or man, but sometimes a couple exchange
tokens. And sometimes gifts are given to a
favorite relative or friend of either sex. Large
or small, any gift given with love expresses the
spirit of the holiday.

Enter Cupid

A mischievous, winged child, armed with darts or a quiver of arrows. His business? The piercing of hearts. Such is Cupid, god of love, and a favorite symbol for Valentine party decorations, candy boxes, or greetings.

Long before there was a Valentine's Day, Cupid played a central role in the ancient Greek and Roman celebrations dedicated to love and lovers. Named *Eros* by the Greeks, the young god was the son and companion of Aphrodite, goddess of love and beauty. Among the Romans the same deity was known as Venus, and her son as Cupid, the name familiar to us today.

By either name, Cupid was a symbol of passionate, tender, or playful love. His arrows were invisible, his targets the hearts of mortals or gods alike. The victim would become aware of having been shot by falling hopelessly, and helplessly, in love.

One lovely myth tells the story of Cupid and the mortal maiden, Psyche. Jealous of Psyche's beauty, Venus ordered Cupid to punish the maiden. Instead, Cupid fell deeply in love at first sight.

38

Sweeping Psyche off to a lovely castle, he made her his bride. As a mortal, however, she was forbidden ever to look at him.

Psyche obeyed willingly and was happy until her sisters paid her a visit. Envious of Psyche's good fortune, they asked, "Where is the husband who keeps you in such splendor? Why can't we see him?"

When Psyche explained that she had never set eyes on him herself, her sisters burst into laughter. "An invisible husband! Who ever heard of that?"

Their taunts ringing in her ears, Psyche could think of nothing else. That evening, in defiance of Cupid's orders, she stole a look at him.

Cupid punished her by departing. The lovely castle and the gardens around it vanished. And Psyche found herself in an open field.

Determined to find her love, she wandered far and wide, never once losing hope. Finally, she came to the temple of Venus.

Wishing to destroy her, the angry love goddess set Psyche a series of tasks, each harder and more dangerous than the one before. For the last task, she gave Psyche a little box. "Take this," she said, "and go down at once to the underworld. Find Proserpine, the wife

of Pluto, and tell her your mistress wants a little of her beauty."

Sure that her end was near, Psyche decided to hasten it. Climbing to a tall tower, she was about to jump when she heard a voice asking why she should give up now after all her bravery. Then she was told how to avoid the dangers of the realm of the dead. Above all, she was not to open the box filled with Proserpine's beauty.

All went well until, on the way back, temptation overcame Psyche and she opened the box. Inside, instead of beauty, was a deadly slumber.

It was Cupid who found her lying lifeless on the ground. Recovered from his hurt, he had been longing to see her. He gathered the sleep from her body, put it back in the box, and touched her with one of his arrows. After a gentle scolding, he explained that it was not for her, a mortal, to discover the secret of the beauty of goddesses.

But Cupid forgave her, and finally Venus relented and forgave her, too. Then the assembled gods, moved by Psyche's undying love for Cupid, made her a goddess.

During the century before the birth of Christ and for a few hundred years afterward, the figure of Cupid appeared in Roman wall paintings. Greek statues of the god were brought to Rome and copied. And many wealthy Romans were laid to rest in stone coffins carved with blissful, sleeping cupids.

A symbol of love since ancient times, Cupid was the natural heir to a holiday when young men "chose" their valentines. Gradually his form altered, and the handsome youth of ancient mythology became the playful cherub we know today.

Like fashions in dress or jewelry, fashions in valentines change, with certain motifs going out of style and others coming in. But whether hovering in the background or playing a starring role, Cupid endures. He, perhaps more than any other single symbol, conveys the light, teasing spirit of St. Valentine's Day.

Valentine Love Birds

From the time of the first valentine, beautiful birds have helped to grace them.

People of the Middle Ages thought that birds chose their mates on St. Valentine's Day. And birds like the missel thrush, the partridge, and the blackbird really did mate in mid-February. From this may have come the idea that all birds did the same.

The 14th century author, Geoffrey Chaucer, spoke of it many times. In his *Parliament of Birds* he wrote:

> For this was on St. Valentine's Day
> When every fowl cometh to choose
> his mate.

A folksong of the time was *The Birds' Wedding,* popular in various versions all over Europe. In the song, doves, nightingales, larks, eagles, or woodpeckers intermarried with wrens, robins, sparrows, or magpies. In German versions, the bride and groom were usually a hen and a rooster.

Among the birds found on valentines, doves have long been favorites—a pair of doves or a single dove, bearing a message.

The dove was sacred to Venus and other love deities. And, from the time of Noah, doves had served as messengers.

42

The turtledove of the Old Testament is usually called, simply, *turtle*. As such it appears in this lovely verse from the *Song of Solomon:*

> The flowers appear on the earth; the time of the singing of *birds* is come, and the voice of the turtle is heard in our land. *SS 2:12*

Some people call the American mourning dove a turtledove. Actually, the turtledove is common in Europe and Asia but never found in North America.

All doves are members of the pigeon family, so they mate for life, sharing the care of their babies. Shy and gentle, they are known for their billing and cooing, and have long been symbols of romantic love.

In many lands, doves were considered magical and were used to divine the future. The heart of a dove was an ingredient in love potions. A white dove flying overhead was said to mean good luck. To dream of a dove was a promise of happiness. Wishes made when the first dove appeared in springtime would come true, or so it was said.

Various groups had various superstitions about these birds. Slaves in the state of Missouri ate a raw dove's heart and pointed downward to win response from the ones they loved.

43

In one of their folksongs are the lines:

Is you a flyin' lark or a settin' dove?
I'se a flyin' lark, my honey love.

A "settin'" dove was a settled married woman. A "flyin'" lark was a single woman.

When printed valentines first appeared, there were special series that featured birds. Toward the end of the 19th century, certain valentines showed pretty girls with clothing made of real feathers. There were even valentines on which a stuffed humming bird, or bird of paradise, was mounted on a satin cushion.

Today, lovebirds, which are really tiny parrots, appear in pairs on some of our valentines. They are an African species, one of the many kinds of parrots found wild in warm climates.

Like parakeets, lovebirds have brilliant feathers in combinations of green, red, blue, orange, and purple. In the wild, they live in pairs, keeping to themselves like couples in love.

As pets, they are lovable, for they are easy to tame and respond to affection. They can even be taught to speak.

Unfortunately, lovebirds can carry a disease harmful to human beings. For this reason, there are strict rules regarding their entry into the country.

Hearts and Sweethearts

In the language of symbols, a red or pink heart, pierced with an arrow, spells Valentine's Day. While other symbols like gloves or tomatoes have come and gone, the heart shape continues, a basic symbol of the holiday of love and romance.

From earliest times, the heart—the most vital organ of a living being—has been held in awe. In most primitive societies, it is believed to contain the soul. The ancient Egyptians thought of it as the source of intelligence.

Today, with the aid of modern science, we know better. Yet we still speak of being "heartsick," or send "heartfelt" greetings to one another, as if our hearts contained, if not our souls, at least our emotions.

Among the ancients, a god or mortal pierced with one of Cupid's arrows suffered the pleasant malady of lovesickness.

Just as Cupid linked himself with a holiday that became ever more romantic, so did Cupid's target—the heart.

Those quick to show their feelings are said to wear their hearts on their sleeves. This saying stems from the medieval custom in England and other parts of Europe of drawing

names of valentines. In some areas the young
men pinned the names of their partners on
their sleeves, and wore them there for at least
a week.

If birds chose partners on St. Valentine's
Day, as people believed, it probably seemed
natural for human beings to do the same.
Young people gathered for the drawing on St.
Valentine's Eve. The names, written on slips
of paper, were drawn from an urn.

When this custom started and how long
it lasted is rather unclear, but in the February
calendar of *Poor Robin's Almanac* for 1670
there appeared a poem beginning:

> Young men and maids, where love
>   combines,
> Each other draw for valentines;
> They clip and kiss, and dance and
>   sing,
> And love like unto anything.

Verses on many English and American
valentines suggest that name drawing continued well into the 19th century, in some

districts at least. On one lovely American rebus valentine are the lines:

Our lots we cast, and thus I drew,
Kind fortune says it must be you.

Of course, plenty of young men found ways of making sure they would draw the names they really wanted.

Young women of the time had customs of their own. A common belief was that the first man seen on Valentine's Day would become one's sweetheart or future husband. One English girl of the 18th century told of staying in bed with her eyes shut until her favorite came to the house.

Some girls wrote the names of boys on slips of paper, wrapped them in clay, and dropped them into water. As the clay fell away, the paper rose to the surface. The first name to arise would be that of her future husband —or so the girl liked to believe.

The idea behind our classroom valentine boxes may be a relic of the time when young men drew the names of their valentines from an urn. The hand drawing out the valentines and reading the names today is often that of a teacher, but he or she is going through the same motions as those young men of long ago.

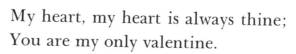

My heart, my heart is always thine;
You are my only valentine.

This inscription from an old English valentine is not much different from those on valentines we send today. Giving one's heart or joining it to someone else's have been valentine themes for centuries.

Valentines in the shape of a heart or with hearts as decoration remain as common as they were when people put loving labor into handmade ones. A rare, round valentine of this kind may be seen in the Metropolitan Museum in New York City. Part of the decoration is a circle of hearts, each one numbered and bearing a message. Message number one reads:

My dear child, I cannot hide my
heart any longer.

This is a cutout valentine with verses in fraktur writing.

Today, not only on valentines does the heart appear over and over. It is also a favorite shape for valentine gifts and goodies. Heart-shaped pins, lockets, earrings, and pendants are popular gifts. And there are heart-shaped cakes, cookies, candies, and lavish red satin heart-shaped boxes, topped with flowers. In a sense, the shape of the heart is the shape of the holiday.

48

Roses Are Red

Sure as the grape grows on the vine
So sure you are my valentine
The rose is red the violet blue
Lilies are fair and so are you.

The red poinsettia has become a symbol of Christmas, and the white lily a symbol of Easter. No one flower by itself stands for Valentine's Day. But a single blossom, a bouquet, or a garland of flowers combines with hearts or cupids to express the essence of the holiday.

Long before there were valentines, flowers served as love tokens on Valentine's Day. And long before there was a Valentine's Day, people linked the beauty and fragrance of flowers with ideas of love and romance. The Greeks and Romans had a love story for almost every kind.

The daisy, the Romans said, had once been a lovely wood nymph. Dancing in a meadow one day, she was seen by Vertumnus, the god of spring, who fell in love with her. When he reached for her, the timid nymph was frightened. So, out of pity, the other gods let her sink into the earth to become the daisy.

49

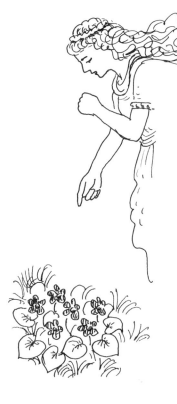

In a story of the violet, Venus was jealous of a group of beautiful maidens. When Cupid refused to say that his mother's beauty was greater than theirs, the goddess became enraged. Beating her rivals until they turned blue, she watched them shrink into violets.

The bachelor's button is also known as cornflower, but in the science of botany the name is *Kyanus*. A Greek youth, Kyanus, was in a field one day, making garlands of the blue blossoms for the altar of Flora, goddess of flowers. When he died, leaving some of the garlands unfinished, Flora was touched, and named the flower after him.

THE QUEEN OF FLOWERS

From the time of Solomon, the flower most closely linked with love has been the rose. It was sacred to Venus and connected with the name of Cupid.

In one myth, Cupid is hurrying off to a council of the gods on Mount Olympus, carrying a vase of nectar for them to drink. When he stumbles and spills the nectar, it bubbles up from the earth in the form of roses.

Another myth offers a reason for the thorns on roses. It seems the lovely flower opened only at the touch of Zephyr, the soft west wind. When Cupid tried to kiss the velvety petals, he was stung by an angry bee hiding within.

To punish the insect, Venus had Cupid string bees along his bowstring. She herself planted their stings along the stem of the flower that had injured Cupid. The stings became thorns, which, ever since, have been a part of roses.

Queen Cleopatra of Egypt, before a visit from her lover, Mark Antony, was said to have covered the floors of her palace with carpets of roses.

Then, as now, throughout the world the rose was the most beloved flower. For a time in between, in the early days of the Christian church, it went out of favor—at least in Rome.

The rose had been sacred to Bacchus, god of wine, as well as to Venus. At banquets for these gods, wealthy Romans had lain on couches spread with rose petals. Around their necks they wore garlands of roses. Chaplets of roses crowned their heads.

Reclining on their beds of roses, they ate, drank, and gossiped. Anything said under the rose—the rose garland hung on the wall or the rose chaplets on their heads—was *sub rosa*,

and supposed to be kept a secret. Meaning *under the rose,* this Latin expression became part of the English language. It is still a common way of describing something to be kept secret.

Roses reminded the Roman church too much of the pagans who had also found entertainment in watching Christians devoured by lions. Later on, the Virgin Mary became the Rose of Heaven, but in early Christian times, the rose was never a symbol of anything holy. As a symbol of love, however, it persisted throughout history.

> And the white rose breathes of love;
> O, the red rose is a falcon,
> And the white rose is a dove.
> —JAMES BOYLE O'REILLY

On valentines of yesterday and today, the rose, usually a red or pink one, holds a place of honor at the side of Cupid.

THE LANGUAGE OF FLOWERS

At different times and in different places, people have used flowers to form a secret language. Each flower had a special meaning. Some flower codes were religious, but the one Charles II of Sweden brought back from the Ottoman Empire in 1714 was romantic.

52

Suiting the mood of the times, it soon spread through the courts of Europe. "Saying it with flowers" became a favorite pastime. Meanings varied but might go something like this:

> *Bleeding heart:* hopeless, but not heartless
> *Gardenia:* I love you in secret
> *Gladiolus:* You pierce my heart
> *Lily-of-the-valley:* Let us make up
> *Rose:* I love you passionately
> *Sweet William:* You are gallant, suave, perfect
> *Violet:* I return your love

Green leaves stood for hope in a love affair. Perhaps this is why British girls used to place bay leaves sprinkled with rose water on their pillows on St. Valentine's Day Eve. They hoped to see in their dreams the faces of their future husbands.

> Good valentine, be kind to me;
> In dreams, let me my true love see.

The flowers on early valentines were usually drawn or painted by hand. Some were pressed flowers, with painted stems and leaves.

One of the glories of the Golden Age of

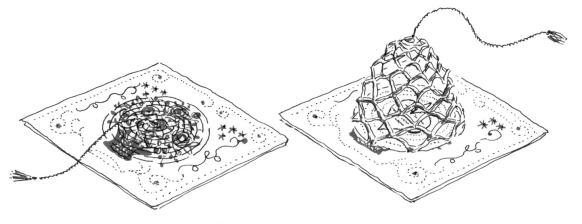

English valentines was the *flower cage,* sometimes called the *cobweb* or *beehive.* The central design was usually a bouquet. Cut into a square or circle of paper threads, it formed a cage when lifted. Through its delicate bars could be seen the picture of a pretty girl or perhaps a cupid.

The roses or other flowers on the flower cage valentines were masterpieces of delicate beauty. At the other extreme were valentines of the 1890's that showed a lady holding a gigantic sunflower with its stout stem and coarse leaves.

In valentine verses, flowers turn up over and over. Many follow the "roses are red" theme. Around 1820, a loyal British subject wrote on his valentine:

> The rose is red, the grass is green,
> God bless you, the King and Queen.

Valentine's Day is a time for saying "I love you," and many men like to say it with flowers. Not only in the United States and England but also in France, Germany, Austria, and Spain, the custom has been spreading.

54

Valentine Lace

Elegant modern valentines often have layers of delicate paper lace, a reminder of the Golden Age of 1840–1860. Heart-shaped candy boxes usually have a lacy border framing the chocolates.

From the days when a knight rode to battle with his lady's scarf or ribbon as a love token, pretty things of this sort have been a symbol of romance.

Lace, so much a part of the romantic holiday, came into being as something lovely to look at rather than something useful. Soft and flattering, the handmade lace of four hundred years ago was instantly popular as a trimming for clothing.

Paper lace was probably first made on the European continent. In England, where valentines were so loved, Joseph Addenbrooke stumbled on a novel way to make it. It was 1834, and he was working for a London paper maker. One day, by accident, a file brushed over a sheet of paper embossed with a raised design. The high points of the design were filed off, leaving tiny holes and a lacelike effect.

The discovery led Addenbrooke into the business of making paper laces, and before

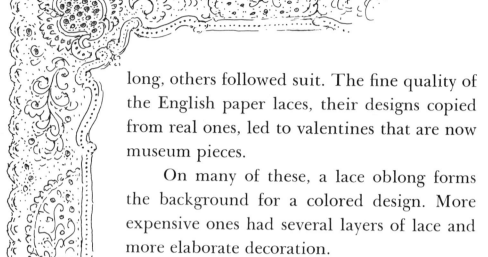

long, others followed suit. The fine quality of the English paper laces, their designs copied from real ones, led to valentines that are now museum pieces.

On many of these, a lace oblong forms the background for a colored design. More expensive ones had several layers of lace and more elaborate decoration.

In the United States, meanwhile, Esther Howland was using the brightly colored bits of paper known as wafers to set off the lace on her valentines.

Card makers in both countries hunted constantly for unusual touches. Gold, silver, and bronze lace appeared. An English novelty was the valentine with a slot to hold a lady's nightcap of real lace. On one of these valentines are the words:

"Goodnight, dear, and in your thoughts forget me not."

Another novelty, sold in 1880 for fifty dollars, was a miniature fire screen edged with genuine lace.

Today, around Valentine's Day, paper lace is still with us, expressing to perfection the frilly nature of the holiday.

Red, Pink, and White

As Valentine's Day nears, shop windows, card racks, and candy counters fill with splashes of red and pink. On party napkins and decorations, and on many valentines, the red or pink is set off by pure white.

Red is a symbol of warmth and feeling. The color of the human heart, it has been a favorite hue for the hearts on valentines of the past and present.

In sending roses to say, "I love you," the first choice is often red. A symbol of love at its most romantic, the red rose graced early valentines as it does today.

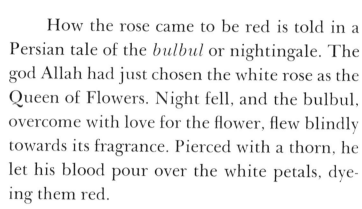

How the rose came to be red is told in a Persian tale of the *bulbul* or nightingale. The god Allah had just chosen the white rose as the Queen of Flowers. Night fell, and the bulbul, overcome with love for the flower, flew blindly towards its fragrance. Pierced with a thorn, he let his blood pour over the white petals, dyeing them red.

Pink, a mixture of red and white, tints roses, rosebuds, and other blossoms on many valentines, old and new. Pink roses or carnations form bright valentine bouquets.

Fashions in color change, and the colors of valentines change with them. So it has been with the color pink, which has ranged from the softest pastel to the boldest magenta.

White, the absence of all color, stands for purity. It appears in the dresses of brides, in their bouquets, their wreaths, and veils. Since St. Valentine's Day is dedicated to courtship, perhaps the bridal veil helped inspire the use of white lace on valentines.

White is also a symbol of faith—on Valentine's Day, a faith betwen two who love each other.

58

Valentine Goodies

Most holidays have special foods, topped off with certain desserts. For Christmas the dessert is plum pudding; for Thanksgiving, pumpkin pie. Valentine's Day foods are all toppings—some kind of sweet, often in the shape of a heart.

At one extreme are hearts weighing five pounds and made of solid chocolate. At the other are the tiny pastel hard-candy hearts, printed with little mottoes.

Valentine mottoes have been with us since the 17th century when Samuel Pepys wrote his famous *Diary*. A man who drew Mrs. Pepys's name drew the motto, "Most courteous and most fair."

Mottoes have changed since then, and those on the tiny sugar hearts are usually silly or flippant. Typical ones are: "You bet!" "Forget it!" and "Me, too!"

Children through the ages have connected holidays with the thought of goodies, but not always with sweets. In times gone by, many children in Europe went hungry. An orange at Christmas or a fresh egg at Easter was a tremendous treat. Around St. Valentine's Day, children looked forward to a currant bun, an apple—or a penny to buy one.

In many towns and villages, bands of children went from house to house, singing:

> Good morning to you, Valentine;
> Curl your locks as I do mine,
> Two before, and three behind.
> Good morning to you, Valentine.

If the children were lucky, the lady of the house would appear with Valentine buns, some fruit, or some pennies.

In some English villages, people gave Valentine buns to their godchildren on the Sunday before and the Sunday after the holiday. The buns were sometimes given to old people as well.

Heart-shaped candies, cookies, and cakes, heart-shaped molds of ice cream, jellies, and puddings—sweets like these seem the perfect choice for a holiday that is itself a delectable topping for all our others.

Nesting birds, mischievous cupids, graceful flowers and heart shapes, lace and ribbons —the Valentine symbols form a kind of endless true-love knot, winding back to the past and into the future.

They suggest that, in spite of wars and world problems of all kinds, romance lives on.

St. Valentine's Day is light and sentimental on the surface. Underneath, like all holidays born of ancient festivals, it expresses something vital:

Winter is winding down. Spring, with its flowers and birdsong, is at last in sight. Birds will mate, as always, and human beings will continue to fall in love and marry. To be alive and a part of all this is truly delightful!

Stories and Poems for Valentine's Day

BREWTON, Sara and John E., compilers. *Sing a Song of Seasons.* Illustrated by Vera Bock. New York: The Macmillan Company, 1955. Includes five Valentine poems, one by Shakespeare and one by Kate Greenaway. For children of about eight to eleven.

BULLA, Clyde. *Valentine Cat.* Illustrated by Leonard Weisgard. New York: Thomas Y. Crowell Company, 1959. A picture-storybook with a cat as hero. For children of eight to eleven.

FISHER, Aileen, compiler. *Skip Around the Year.* Illustrated by Gioia Fiammenghi. New York: Thomas Y. Crowell Company, 1967. Includes such conservation-oriented poems as one that suggests spreading seeds for birds on St. Valentine's Day. For children from kindergarten to grade three.

HAYS, Wilma P. *The Story of Valentine.* Illustrated by Leonard Weisgard. New York: Coward, McCann & Geoghegan, Inc., 1956. The story of the "real" St. Valentine, emphasizing qualities of courage and faith. For children of about eight to eleven.

LARRICK, Nancy, selector. *Poetry for Holidays.* Champaign, Illinois: Garrard Publishing Company, 1968. Includes several poems for St. Valentine's Day. Suitable for children of elementary school age.

LOVELACE, Maud Hart. *The Valentine Box.* Illustrated by Ingrid Fetz. New York: Thomas Y. Crowell Company, 1966. A small black girl, new to the community, makes friends via the classroom Valentine box. For children of seven to ten.

MILHOUS, Katherine. *Appolonia's Valentine.* Illustrated by the author. New York: Charles Scribner's Sons, 1954. A picture-storybook about children in a small Pennsylvania school who are making cut-out valentines. For storytellers or for children of six to ten to read to themselves. Will inspire the making of valentines.

62

Sources

BULFINCH, Thomas. *Bulfinch's Mythology.* New York: Thomas Y. Crowell Company.

BUTLER, Alban. *Lives of the Saints.* Beverly Hills, Calif.: Benziger, Inc., 1926.

CHAMBERS, Robert, editor. *Book of Days.* Detroit: Gale Research Co., 1967 [Repr. of 1886 ed.].

FARJEON, Eleanor. *The New Book of Days.* New York: Henry Z. Walck, Inc., 1961.

FRAZER, James G. *The Golden Bough.* New York: St. Martin's Press, Inc., 1914.

HAZELTINE, Mary E. *Anniversaries and Holidays.* 2nd. Ed. Chicago: American Library Association, 1944.

HOLLINGSWORTH, Buckner. *Flower Chronicles.* New Brunswick, N.J.: Rutgers University Press, 1958.

JAMES, Edwin O. *Seasonal Feasts and Festivals.* New York: Barnes and Noble, 1963.

JONES, Gertrude. *Dictionary of Mythology, Folklore, and Symbols.* Metuchen, N.J.: Scarecrow Press, Inc., 1962.

LEACH, Maria, editor. *Funk & Wagnalls Standard Dictionary of Folklore, Mythology, and Legend.* New York: Funk & Wagnalls, 1972.

LEE, Ruth Webb. *A History of Valentines.* Wellesley Hills, Mass.: Lee Publications, 1952.

LEHNER, Ernst and Johanna. *Folklore and Symbolism of Flowers, Plants and Trees.* New York: Tudor Publishing Company, 1960.

SKINNER, Charles M. *Myths and Legends of Flowers, Trees, Fruits and Plants, in all Ages and all Climes.* Philadelphia: J. B. Lippincott Co., 1925.

STAFF, Frank. *The Valentine and its Origin.* New York/Washington, D.C.: Praeger Publishers, Inc., 1969.

WRIGHT, Arthur R. *British Calendar Customs, Vol. II.* Craus Reprints, 1968.

Index